YOUR KNOWLEDGE HAS VALUE

- We will publish your bachelor's and master's thesis, essays and papers

- Your own eBook and book - sold worldwide in all relevant shops

- Earn money with each sale

Upload your text at www.GRIN.com and publish for free

Bibliographic information published by the German National Library:

The German National Library lists this publication in the National Bibliography; detailed bibliographic data are available on the Internet at http://dnb.dnb.de .

Imprint:

Copyright © 2019 GRIN Verlag
Print and binding: Books on Demand GmbH, Norderstedt Germany
ISBN: 9783668946095

This book at GRIN:

https://www.grin.com/document/469097

Alexandra Kurcikova

Reflections on social development and values in Victorian England as depicted in Jane Eyre

How did Religion and Gender shape a society?

GRIN Verlag

GRIN - Your knowledge has value

Since its foundation in 1998, GRIN has specialized in publishing academic texts by students, college teachers and other academics as e-book and printed book. The website www.grin.com is an ideal platform for presenting term papers, final papers, scientific essays, dissertations and specialist books.

Visit us on the internet:

http://www.grin.com/

http://www.facebook.com/grincom

http://www.twitter.com/grin_com

Vorwissenschaftliche Arbeit

Eine Reflexion sozialer Entwicklungen und Werte
im Viktorianischen England
am Beispiel des Romans Jane Eyre

Reflections on social development and values in Victorian England as depicted in Jane Eyre

How did gender and religion shape a society?

Alexandra Kurcikova

8A

22. Februar 2019

Abstract

Jane Eyre, one of the most significant novels of the Victorian Era, provides reflections on the period and its society. This paper examines the changes and developments of Victorian England. It further deals with the literary situation and places Charlotte Brontë's novel Jane Eyre in its historical context. After a short summary, there follows an examination of the issues Jane Eyre revolts against. Her criticism against the then accepted gender roles and her liberal idea of womanhood indicate a strong female emancipation. Through an interpretation of certain passages, Jane's demand for equality of gender becomes evident. Jane Eyre also reflects on Victorian morality and people's idea of religion. The most important Christian conventions are presented illustrated by characters matching those different interpretations of Christianity. The then often valid severity in faith is against Jane's idea of a good and loving God.

1 Introduction

Jane Eyre – one woman reflecting on society.

Charlotte Brontë's celebrated novel is truly one of a kind. It portrays a young woman who speaks up against the injustice and mistreatment of many aspects given during the Victorian Era. This is not surprising, as the duration of Queen Victoria's reign was a time of change and innovation. The Victorian period witnessed a great boost in its economy as well as alterations of its social structure: The Industrial Revolution stimulated globalisation as well as modern science. Then, the emergence of pre-feminism, with criticism focusing on reforming the then accepted gender roles. Christianity was also re-thought and liberalised. The list could, of course, go on for pages. The primary aim of this paper will be, however, to examine some of the changes and developments which are directly portrayed in Jane Eyre.

- Which conditions were given during Queen Victoria's reign?

- What influenced the Victorians' morality? Which values emerged/were preserved?

- What characterises Victorian literature?

- Does Jane Eyre correspond with the changes during the Victorian Era?

- Does Jane Eyre approve of the then valid social situation?

- **What is the nature of her revolt?**

In order to have these questions answered, this paper will be split into three major parts. Firstly, a historical context will be established. Then, using the method of literary interpretation of Jane Eyre, the paper will be split into two major topics:

Gender and Religion.

These two aspects seem most relevant in Jane Eyre and are also amongst the most important conditions that shaped Victorian society. At this point an analysis of some of the novel's characters will be necessary. After the literary examination it will become evident what it was like living in Victorian England and why this period underwent so many revolts and reforms.

2 The Victorian Era

2.1 Period overview

Scarcely any other era in British history, brought as many social, economic and politic changes as the Victorian Era. It has long been a tradition to categorise British history in certain time durations, eras, named after their current heads of state. Thus, Princess Alexandrina Victoria of Kent (later; Queen) became the eponym of her time when she ascended to the throne in 1837. The full duration of her reign lasted until her death in 1901, marking the end to the Victorian Period. The Victorian society was witness of many innovations, setting the 19th century in great contrast with its predecessor, the Regency Era.[1]

It is important to mention some of the reforms and acts implemented by the 19th century government, to establish context for the further discussion of Victorian society. The first Great Reform Act of 1832 (of which there were three during Queen Victoria's Age), for instance, widened the franchise to a considerably greater part of the population. By the late Victorian years, however, still only around 12 per cent of the population were legally allowed to vote. Women altogether were excluded from the extension of the right to vote until the year 1918, due the success of the suffragette movement. In fact, women's liberty was strictly limited throughout the century, making them almost completely dependent on their male superiors (fathers, brothers, husbands). This custom goes under the name of "coverture" and was effectively annulled by the Married Women's Property Act of 1882. Furthermore, the Victorians (foremost those that were poverty-stricken) were made to suffer under the Poor Law Act of 1834, which condemned them to be placed in workhouses and similar institutions, which were known for their catastrophic conditions famously displayed and criticised by Charles Dickens's novels. One progressive achievement of the Victorian Period was passed by William Wilberforce's anti-slavery administration

---

[1] cf. Erzgräber, Bernhard/Fabian, Kurt et al. (1991): Die Englische Literatur, Epochen, Formen. Munich: Deutscher Taschenbuch Verlag, p. 153.

that brought about the abolition of slavery, liberating thousands of colonial slaves, in the year 1833.[2]

The Empire's economy saw a huge shift from an agricultural oriented policy to, as Sean Purchase puts it, "an urban and industrial society, based on an increasing culture of individualism and capitalism".[3] Britain was advancing and consciously heading for a new modern age. Manufacturers, industrialists, and entrepreneurs were encouraged by the new capitalist spirit, seeking profit and thus gradually gaining on power, influence, and foremost status. The middle-class, consisting mostly of such tradesmen's families, emerged. Technological progress, such as the construction of the railway, operated by a steam engine, led towards an Industrial Revolution that spread across all Great Britain. Scientific discoveries were made and supported, with Prince Albert himself exhibiting British scientific and technological achievements in the Great Exhibition in 1851, which held over 6 million visitors. The new interest in sciences resulted in a reorganisation of Victorian morals. A suitable example of this is Charles Darwin's Evolution Theory, which made the Victorian people question long-standing doctrines of the church.[4]

Thus, it can be said that the Victorian Age was a time of great prosperity, showing itself in the vast population growth that rose up to 30 million by Queen Victoria's death in 1901. The then well-known historian Walter Besant summarised his progressive generation thus:

> To us, who find it difficult to stand outside and consider events in their true proportion, the period seems like a grand triumphal march. [...] The changes are nothing short of a transformation. And no one regrets the change. During this long period there has arisen in the national mind such a spirit of enterprise, endeavour and achievement as has n parallel in our history except in the reign of Queen Elizabeth. Now, as then, people have been restless: this restlessness has shown itself in colonisation, in emigration, in research, in discovery, in invention – in changes of every kind.[5]

The economic upheaval affected the Victorians' idea of values directly. The welfare of a large portion of Britain's inhabitants, as well as the Education Act of

---

[2] cf. Purchase, Sean (2006): Key Concepts in Victorian Literature. New York: Palgrave Macmillian, (Palgrave Key Concepts: Literature), pp. 3.
[3] Ibid., p. 3.
[4] cf. Ibid., p. 122.
[5] Besant, Walter (1897): Jubilee Portrait of our Queen. In: Illustrated London News. Diamond Jubilee number. p. 1.

1870 making school compulsory, thus that creating better-educated Victorians (from which the "polished" middle-class mostly benefited), steered people's conscience towards ethical questions. Social evils, moral queries, and gender roles were reconsidered. Many written critiques in form of literature, speeches, arts etc. followed.[6] Michael Paterson fittingly described this development by commenting:

> Within the sixty-four years between 1837 and 1901 spanned by Victoria's reign [...] the British developed into a gentler, more generous, more civilized people than their uncouth Georgian grandfathers had been (by the fifties animal-baiting had been banned; [...] transportation and public hangings ceased; and flogging was abolished [...] The Victorians hated the moral laxity of the Georgians as much as they found their manners and ideas passé. The sheer scale of Victorian buildings, ships, bridges or railway networks made everything that had gone before seem small and parochial by comparison.[7]

3 Victorian literature

3.1 Victorian readership

Relating to the chapter above, we have seen that Victorian society has undergone a certain "refinement", primarily in its education. An example of this is the establishment of the well-esteemed middle-class, who sought to manifest their status by keeping up with the current intellect. Consequently, an increase in the interest in arts followed with the novel being most prominent amongst these. This new thirst for literature was acknowledged and met by provision of countless papers, magazines, and novels. The increase in the sheer amount of published works through the discovery of new printing techniques, lowering the overall cost of books, was also a reason why reading gained on popularity. As the century continued, reading was for the first time not primarily exercised for intellectual reasons of learning and self-improvement, but as a leisure activity. Small "pocket-editions" of great literary works could be carried around everywhere. The railway added to the demand of books, with long train journeys being a convenient opportunity to read. Train stations were now housing bookstalls, where people could purchase prose, poetry, and papers of their choice. Special book editions

---

[6] cf. Paterson, Michael (2008): Life in Victorian Britain. A Social History of Queen Victoria's Reign. London: Robinson pp. 14.
[7] Ibid., p. 15.

like the "Railway Library" were introduced chiefly for train passengers. Furthermore, libraries were being erected everywhere, the 1841-built London Library (initiated by Thomas Carlyle) being an example of this. With more readers there came along more writers. The 19th century saw the emergence of, authors celebrated until today such as Charles Dickens, Thomas Hardy, Anthony Trollope, George Eliot, and of course the Brontë sisters.[8]

3.2 The Victorian novel

Compared to the Romantic Period during which the literally genre of poetry gained on significance, the Victorian Society set more store by prose, more specifically; the novel. There are several reasons to explain the novels' vogue amongst the Victorians, but they all share a certain component: The Victorian Novel reflected the ever-present social and economic changes society had to undergo. The sheer complexity of sociological and economic transitions of the Victorian Age, made it impossible for anything but prose to reflect on these changes, by it being a longer form of literature enabling an author to provide a more detailed picture of their time. Moreover, novels mirrored the very issue of social existence during the 19th century. Authors of that time often expressed to have the urge to outpoint social evils, bring an industrial, fast moving society back to its morals. The catastrophic working-class conditions were written about, others specialised e.g. on pre-feminist and feminist writing, proposing the so-called Woman Question. This question consisted of a widespread debate about the place of women in society. Moreover, Victorian novels distinctly show evidence of how capitalism had made the middle class the most influential class of the Age. This middle-class was primarily responsible for publishing, and reading literature, hence that these topics reflected the middle-class's perspective on society. It is altogether impossible to characterise the "typical" Victorian novel, as the Victorian Era lasted over 60 years, there can however be remarked that many of these works follow the literary genre of realism.[9] Charlotte Brontë herself, phrased a desire to portray realism in the first chapter of her 1849 published novel Shirley by writing:

---

[8] Paterson, Life in Victorian Britain, pp. 279.
[9] Purchase, Key Concepts in Victorian Literature, pp. 145.

If you think, from this prelude, that anything like a romance is preparing for you, reader, you never were more mistaken. Do you anticipate sentiment, and poetry, and reverie? Do you expect passion, and stimulus, and melodrama? Calm your expectations; reduce them to a lowly standard. Something real, cool, and solid, lies before you; something unromantic as Monday morning, when all who have work wake with the consciousness that they must rise and betake themselves thereto. It is not positively affirmed that you shall not have a taste of the exciting, perhaps towards the middle and close of the meal, but it is resolved that the first dish set upon the table shall be one that a Catholic––ay, even an Anglo-Catholic––might eat on Good Friday in Passion Week: it shall be cold lentiles and vinegar without oil; it shall be unleavened bread with bitter herbs and no roast lamb.[10]

It is however remarkable, that her preceding novel Jane Eyre, which is the subject of this paper, is full of romantic elements and melodrama. How is this controversy to be explained? Critic Margaret Anne Doody breaks this issue down by arguing that critical practice and literary history of the 19th century, focused too much on realism while many writers adhered to a broader tradition of romance, fantasy etc.[11]

This seems to be the case with Charlotte Brontë. Although she was definitely influenced by realism she did not confine herself to that style only, often combining both realistic and romantic elements. Her novel Jane Eyre is obviously a romantic novel that does not fail to outpoint the Victorian "reality", its centre theme being social inequality in status, gender and religion.

---

[10] Brontë, Charlotte (2007): Shirley. Oxford/New York: Oxford University Press, 2007, p. 44.
[11] quoted from (cf.): Roberts, Adam (2003): Victorian Culture and Society. London: Arnold, (The Essential Glossary series), p. 184.

4 Jane Eyre

4.1 Publication

After its publication in 1847, Jane Eyre instantly received positive reviews. Due to an oppression of female artists, Charlotte published her novel under the pseudonym Currer Bell, in order to hide her sex. Thus, her work could be read with sufficient seriousness. After she publicly admitted to being the author of Jane Eyre, however, the responses became much more severe. Seeking professional opinion, Charlotte wrote to poet laureate Robert Southey, asking him what he thought about Jane Eyre.[12] His answering letter contained harsh criticism:

> Literature cannot be the business of a woman's life, and it ought not to be, the more she is engaged in her proper duties, the less leisure will she have for it, even as an accomplishment and a recreation.[13]

This close-mindedness and suppression of the female gender is exactly what Charlotte criticises and revolts against in her novel Jane Eyre. Her constant request is equality of gender. Jane's relationship with her master Mr Rochester, her passionate nature, and the fact that she freely expresses her thoughts was altogether contradictory to the idea of womanhood in Victorian England.[14]

4.2 Plot

Jane Eyre, Charlotte Brontë's first novel, approaches the social situation of early Victorian England by portraying a young governess and her struggle for autonomy. The work can be assigned to the category of 'bildungsroman'. Oxford Dictionary defines a bildungsroman by it being "a novel dealing with one person's formative years or spiritual education".[15]

---

[12] Cf. Bertolino, Paola (2001/2002): Female emancipation in Charlotte Bronte's Jane Eyre. Seminar paper. University of Leipzig, p. 10.
[13] Quoted from: Ibid. p.10
[14] Cf. Ibid., p.10
[15] Oxford Dictionary (2019): Bildungsroman. URL:
https://en.oxforddictionaries.com/definition/bildungsroman (accessed February 17th 2019)

Jane Eyre, the novel's protagonist, is an orphan who lives with her aunt Reed and her children at Gateshead. There she is deprived of all affection, as her cruel cousins terrorise her and aunt Reed thinks her an intruder upon the family. As the situation at Gateshead escalates her aunt sends her to Lowood school, a charitable institution where she receives an education. The standards at Lowood school are, however, devastating and Jane suffers from constant cold, lack of food, the spreading of sickness and, foremost, humiliation. These low standards are due to the institution's severe manager, Mr Brocklehurst, a clergyman. At Lowood school Jane encounters her first ever friend Helen Burns, who deeply influences her spiritual life. Helen soon dies of typhus, and Jane is again left friendless. Throughout her stay at Lowood, Jane grows into an independent and intelligent woman.

Seeking to see a bit of the world, Jane advertises for a position as a governess and receives one at Thornfield Hall. She tutors Adèle, a little French girl who is Mr Rochester's warden. Mr Rochester, the master of Thornfield Hall, for whom Jane develops feelings, is a severe and melancholic man. They immediately form a bond through their intellectual and sometimes bizarre conversations. Despite their evident difference in rank, Mr Rochester asks her to marry him. On the day of their wedding, however, Jane discovers that he is already married to a West-Indian woman named Bertha Mason (- Rochester). Bertha is mentally ill and therefore locked up inside one of the rooms at Thornfield, with Grace Pool constantly overseeing her. At this discovery the marriage is halted and Jane flees from Thronfield without any idea where to go and with no finances.

She is admitted to a house by St John Rivers, again a member of the clergy, with whose sisters, Mary and Diana, Jane soon becomes good friends. St John also provides her with a teaching post at a small local school. After a year, he informs Jane about his plans of travelling to India and becoming a missionary there. He asks her to accompany him on his journey as his wife. Jane cannot accept this marriage as she does not love St John.

To her surprise, Jane's uncle bequeaths her with a considerable inheritance, making her financially independent. At this point Jane realises her continuing love for Mr Rochester and decides to return to Thornfield Hall. At her arrival she finds the place destroyed. After some inquiry she receives information that there was a terrible fire at Thornfield set by Mr Rochester's wife Bertha, who is now dead. Jane finds a crippled and blind Mr Rochester, who has undergone a spiritual transformation, living not far from his original estate, and they finally marry – being equals.

5 Gender

5.1 Gender in the Victorian Era

During the Victorian Era women were obstructed by a male-centred society which allowed them explicitly limited personal and social autonomy. This circumstance is based on the assumption that women differ from men in many crucial aspects. In comparison to men's naturally given physical strength, women were considered to be gentle, docile and essentially weak creatures. Their identity was marked by their servitude displayed towards their husbands and male superiors.[16] Philosopher John Burgon in 1884 fittingly described the situation by saying:

> "Woman's strength lies in her essential weakness. [...] Removed from the stifling atmosphere in which perforce the battle of life has to be fought out by the rougher sex, - she is, what she was intended to be – the one solace of man's life, his chiefest joy."[17]

Thus, the idea emerged that women's prime function was to be men's conscience and their great strength lay in the pureness of their spirit. Another significant aspect is the belief that the female sex is incapable of experiencing passion and or any deep emotion at all. Combined with the denial of woman's ability to be perceptive of higher education, those circumstances led to a general captivity of the female gender. [18]

5.1.1 Legal situation

The law stated the position of women as well. During the 19th century, just like during the 18th century, women were legally considered man's property. They first belonged to their fathers and then husbands (or brothers if the woman remained unmarried). They were considered completely inferior to the male gender. Thus, Victorian women had practically no possibility of gaining autonomy for themselves. Only marriage gave them the chance to earn status, and consequently

---

[16] Cf. Wilhelm, Beate (2005): The Role of Women in Victorian England reflected in Jane Eyre. Seminar paper. Albert-Ludwigs Universität Freiburg, p. 4.
[17] Burstyn, Joan N. (1980): Victorian education and the ideal of womenhood. London: Croom and Helm Ltd, p. 33.
[18] Cf. Wilhelm, The Role of Women in Victorian England reflected in Jane Eyre, p. 4.

find a place for themselves amongst society. Marriage was therefore aspired by nearly all Victorian women. Furthermore, they had no right to own property, no rights over their children and received only shallow education. This poor education was primarily focused on preparing them for marriage. Moreover, they were not allowed to divorce their husbands, no matter what their circumstances were.[19]

5.1.2 Tasks

It follows that men's and women's daily tasks were likewise clearly distinguished. While men were expected to earn a living, hence provide for their wives, sisters and children – women's tasks consisted mainly of domestic duties and were performed inside the household. Accordingly, they were to oversee the education of their children, do the shopping, organise the household and generally provide tranquillity when their husbands came home. They were to ensure a peaceful and comfortable family home. A woman in the Victorian Era who was completely absorbed in household affaires and not working secured her husband's status amongst society. The more successful the husband was the more leisure a woman could afford. However, amongst the middle class there were women who had to earn their own money, and therefore were wholly dependent on their employment. Those women originated from socially deprived families and were looked upon with contempt. They often took up the position of governesses. Thus, they had to be provided with a thorough education, which many were sceptical of. [20]

5.1.3 Governesses

Middle-class women living in the Victorian period, either remained at home and cared for their husbands and children or were in employment. If they were married, they often took up the positions of servants, if they were unmarried, they were left with two options: either writing or working as governesses. Both these options were still looked upon with contempt by many fellow Victorians. The

---

[19] Cf. Kolle, Therese Cecilie (2011): Woman's struggle for autonomy. A reading of Jane Eyre, Wuthering Heights and The Mill on the Floss. MA Thesis. University of Oslo, p. 12.
[20] Cf. Wilhelm, The Role of Women in Victorian England reflected in Jane Eyre, p. 4.

Brontë sisters, of course, present a most fitting example. They all dedicated their lives to producing literature, but also had experience of being governesses.[21] As Cornelia Peters states, "an 1851 census lists 25,000 governesses in the United Kingdom, as opposed to 750,000 female domestic servants."[22]

The social status of a governess was often quite contradictory. Many conflicts arose out of a difficulty to properly place a governess inside a home. While a governess was a woman of the same or sometimes even higher social class than the family she worked for, she nevertheless occupied the position of a domestic servant.[23] This resulted in a common mistreatment of governesses by the masters and mistresses she worked for. Their pupils following suit, they often disrespected their governesses.[24] This becomes evident in chapter 17, when Blanche Ingram openly ridicules her own governess's performance by saying:

> I have just one word to say of the whole tribe; they are a nuisance. Not that I ever suffered much from them; I took care to turn the tables. What tricks Theodore and I used to play on our Miss Wilsons, and Mrs. Greys, and Madame Jouberts! [...] The best fun was with Madame Joubert: [...] I see her yet in her raging passions, when we had driven her to extremities — spilt our tea, crumbled our bread and butter, tossed our books up to the ceiling, and played a charivari with the ruler and desk, the fender and fire-irons. Theodore, do you remember those merry days? [25]

A governess was to carry out tasks and duties of a lady and a mother, "but without their social gratification".[26] Sexual desires were naturally intolerable, and their personal leisure time was limited to two to three hours a day. Due to these many repressions and oppressions, it is not very surprising that many governesses suffered from mental illnesses. A large number of them developed nervous irritability, which is more commonly known as classical hysteria. As a consequence, they were sent to lunatic asylums, where it was common to lock them up under constant watch of a nurse. This is the way Mr Rochester treats his wife's insanity. Today's psychological standards allow us to deduce that what these governesses were suffering from were mere psychosomatic illnesses, which

---

[21] Cf. Khan, Tahir Amin (2017): Social classes in Victorian Era. In: International Journal of Advanced Engineering and Research Development. Vol. 4. Iss. 7, p. 516.
[22] Cf. Peters, Cornelia (2016): Gender roles in Charlotte Brontë's "Jane Eyre". Seminar paper. University of Koblenz-Landau, p. 16.
[23] Cf. Wilhelm, The Role of Women in Victorian England reflected in Jane Eyre, p. 8.
[24] Cf. Ibid., p. 8.
[25] Brontë, Charlotte (2006): Jane Eyre. London: Penguin Group,, pp. 205.
[26] Peters, Gender roles in Charlotte Brontë's "Jane Eyre", p. 17.

originated from the repression forced upon these women. Throughout the Victorian Era, however, mental illness was said to stem from women's weak nature and their unstable reproductive system.[27]

5.2 Progressive Jane

5.2.1 Jane as a governess

Jane's position as a governess luckily bypasses many of those repressions, as they are mentioned above. Thornfield Hall, the name of the residence she is employed at, is the home of Mr Rochester, who is its only master, so Jane has no mistress to rival with. Her only student is no "self-confident English heiress"[28], but Adele, a French orphan and Mr Rochester's warden. Her relationship with Adele is friendly, but nonetheless a little distant. Jane does not agree with the wide-spread assumption about the "solemn doctrines about the angelic nature of children"[29] nor the "idolatrous devotion"[30] that was expected of a governess. Their relationship is close enough "to make us both content in each other's society".[31] After the catastrophic standards of Lowood school, Thornfield Hall seems very well appointed. Nevertheless, Jane remains restless and dissatisfied with her current life. This discontentment is expressed by a series of thoughts, which are entirely incompatible with the mindset of most English governesses[32]:

> [...] then I longed for a power of vision which might overpass that limit; which might reach the busy world, towns, regions full of life I had heard of but never seen--that then I desired more of practical experience than I possessed; more of intercourse with my kind, of acquaintance with variety of character, than was here within my reach. I valued what was good in Mrs. Fairfax, and what was good in Adele; but I believed in the existence of other and more vivid kinds of goodness, and what I believed in I wished to behold.[33]

This longing for a life of opportunity does not only surpass the horizon of a common Victorian governess it is more than even a lady from the upper class could hope for. Jane inwardly protests against a humble, tranquil life of a

---

[27] Cf. Ibid., p. 17.
[28] Ibid., p. 17.
[29] Brontë, Jane Eyre, p. 128
[30] Ibid., p. 128.
[31] Ibid., p. 128.
[32] Cf. Peters, Gender roles in Charlotte Brontë's "Jane Eyre", p. 18.
[33] Brontë, Jane Eyre, p. 129.

governess full of sexual repression. Jane also criticises the restrictions forced upon Victorian women, like their supposed incapability of being perceptive of more profound education.[34]

5.3 Feminist Jane

5.3.1 Equality

There have been many disputes over whether or not Jane Eyre is a feminist novel. According to the Oxford Dictionary the term 'feminism' means "The advocacy of women's rights on the ground of the equality of the sexes".[35] This definition completely corresponds with Jane Eyre, as she herself supports equality of gender. Critic Robert B. Martin argues in the same way:

> Miss Bronte asks only for the simple [...] recognition that the same heart and the same spirit animate both men and women, and that love is the pairing of equals in these spheres. [...] The famous plea that women ought not to be confined "to making pudding and knitting stockings, to playing on the piano and embroidering bags" [in Chap. 12] is not propaganda for equal employment but for a recognition of woman's emotional nature. [...] Only equals like Jane and Rochester dare to speak truth couched in language of unadorned directness.[36]

It can be therefore concluded that on the basis of requesting equality of gender, Jane Eyre is indeed a feminist novel. Moreover, Jane Eyre, has often been mentioned as the first feminist work of importance. Her is supported by one of the most insightful passages in chapter 8:

> Women are supposed to be very calm generally: but women feel just as men feel; they need exercise for their faculties, and a field for their efforts as much as their brothers do; they suffer from too rigid a restraint, too absolute a stagnation, precisely as men would suffer; and it is narrow-minded in their more privileged fellow-creatures to say that they ought to confine themselves to making puddings and knitting stockings, to playing on the piano and embroidering bags. It is thoughtless to condemn them, or laugh at them, if they seek to do more or learn more than custom has pronounced necessary for their sex.[37]

Dissenters might argue that Jane walks the conventional path that was expected of women, as she clearly honours marriage. It is her attitude, however, with which

---

[34] Cf. Peters, Gender roles in Charlotte Brontë's "Jane Eyre", p. 18.
[35] Oxford Dictionary: Feminism. URL: https://en.oxforddictionaries.com/definition/feminism (accessed February 14th 2019)
[36] Quoted from: De Groot, Caroline (2008): "Equal we are" - Jane Eyre Versus the Victorian Woman. Seminar paper. Université catholique de Louvain, p. 9.
[37] Brontë, Jane Eyre, p. 217.

she walks the conventional path. The next chapters will present text specimens, which contain Jane's feminist mindset.

5.3.2 Marriage to Mr Rochester: Independence

Although Jane values marriage, she feels sceptical about being financially dependent on her husband-to-be Mr Rochester. She fears losing her independence through entering an unequal partnership with her master. During her stay at Thornfield Hall, Mr Rochester clearly superior, as he has "financial power over Jane, the power of knowledge and the physical power of masculinity, along with far more rights."[38]

Even when she accepts to marry Mr Rochester, she insists on keeping her position as a governess and receiving regular payment.[39] What she desires above all is complete equality, from which her marriage cannot be excluded:

> I am not talking to you now through the medium of custom, conventionalities, nor even of mortal flesh; - it is my spirit that addresses your spirit; just as if both had passed through the grave, and we stood at God's feet, equal,- as we are![40]

Only at the end of the novel they can finally get married, as Jane is finally independent from Mr Rochester. Her spiritual growth as well as the fact that she is now an heiress, establish equality between them. Metaphorically Mr Rochester's blindness allows him to perceive Jane for what she really is; a spiritually and financially independent equal.[41]

> 'What, Janet! Are you an independent woman? A rich woman?'
> 'Quite rich, sir. If you won't let me live with you, I can build a house of my own close up to your door, and you may come and sit in my parlour when you want company of an evening.'
> 'But as you are rich, Jane, you have now, no doubt, friends who will look after you, and not suffer you to devote yourself to a blind lamenter like me?'
> 'I told you I am independent, sir, as well as rich: I am my own mistress.'[42]

---

[38] Wilhelm, The Role of Women in Victorian England reflected in Jane Eyre, p. 8.
[39] Cf. Ibid., p. 14.
[40] Brontë, Jane Eyre, p. 292.
[41] Cf. Wilhelm, The Role of Women in Victorian England reflected in Jane Eyre, p. 14.
[42] Brontë, Jane Eyre, p. 501.

5.3.3 Lowood School: Oppression against women

Within Lowood School, we see Helen Burns being forced to endure constant submission and seeking refuge in religion.[43] This submission portrays the constant oppression directed towards Victorian women at that time. In chapter 6 Jane openly marvels at Helen's patience with oppression:

> 'But then it seems disgraceful to be flogged, and to be sent to stand in the middle of a room full of people; and you are such a great girl: I am far younger and I could not bear it.'
> 'Yet it would be your duty to bear it, if you could not avoid it: It is weak and silly to say you cannot bear what it is your fate to be required to bear.'[44]

Jane evidently struggles to fathom the acceptance of injustice and persistence in tranquillity exercised by Helen. She herself is sensitive and passionate and compelled to revolt against abuse and brutality used against her. Another example of this is the red-room scene in Chapter 2.

5.3.4 Red room scene: Submission and stillness

Jane is actively mistreated by her superior male cousin, and after an attempt of defending herself she is locked up in a mysterious room. She is punished for her revolt by being forced to 'sit still', bound to a chair with a pair of female garters. A situation metaphorically demonstrating a fate Victorian women had to endure; Indifference, ignorance, submission and forced stillness.[45] Aunt Read further humiliates her with a warning that "it's on only on condition of perfect submission and stillness that I shall liberate you then."[46]

---

[43] Cf. Wilhelm, The Role of Women in Victorian England reflected in Jane Eyre, p. 14.
[44] Brontë, Jane Eyre, p. 66.
[45] Cf. Wilhelm, The Role of Women in Victorian England reflected in Jane Eyre, p. 5.
[46] Brontë, Jane Eyre, p.21.

6 Religion

6.1 Influence of Christianity

Another main theme mentioned and criticised in Jane Eyre is religion. To Charlotte Brontë herself, religion is one of the most important values in life. She does not hesitate to outline her own personal experience and opinion on the religious practice of the 19th century in Jane Eyre. Throughout the novel we encounter many different Christian approaches displayed by e.g. Mr. Brocklehurst, St. John Rivers, Helen Burns etc. Many contemporary critics, however, accused the novel of being irreligious and Charlotte Brontë's religious criticism of being offensive towards the church. Understanding Jane Eyre's critical examination of early-Victorian religion and religious institutions is a crucial key to understanding the novel properly. In order to establish a general picture of faith and religion in the Victorian Era, it is necessary to point out several religious movements that spread throughout England.[47]

Due to great progress both in science and economy, Victorian society began to question long-standing doctrines of the church. Doubt was expressed against the church and its religious tradition both in private and in public. Charles Darwin's evolution theory, which provided an alternative explanation of the origin of life, as well as the new German higher criticism of the bible (a series of biblical papers that emerged in German scientific circles in late years of the 18th century) made many people waver in their faith. Historian J. Hillis Miller introduced the phrase "the disappearance of God"[48] as a synonym for this development. Religious doubt soon became a topic many 19th century writers settled upon. While many rejected Christianity entirely, this criticism caused a new religious renewal in others. A large number of people spoke up to defend their faith, others held on to their religion as a traditional value in a time they felt was immoral. Christianity was nonetheless undergoing a transformation.[49]

---

[47] Cf. VanZanten Gallagher, Susan (2001): Jane Eyre and Christianity. In: Long Hoeveler, Diane/Lau, Beth: et al. (Ed.): Approaches to Teaching Charlotte Brontë's Jane Eyre. New York: The Modern Language Association of America. (Approaches to Teaching World Literature), p. 62.
[48] Quoted from: Ibid., p. 62.
[49] Cf. Ibid., p. 62.

This transformation had already begun with the Methodist Movement of the 18th century, led by the then well-known preacher John Wesley. Their number continued to grow even until the early 19th century. After the French Revolution, however, Methodism was beginning to be associated with anti-authoritarian and revolutionary links, losing many of its supporters.[50]

People's attention turned towards another religious movement within the Anglican church itself: Evangelicalism. The evangelical tradition, distinct from Methodism, called for religious reform and a new practical piety. By the late 1850 Evangelicalism was widely accepted throughout England, and their charitable work for the oppressed brought about many reforms in workhouses, prisons and the anti-slave-movement. Critic Elisabeth Jay goes as far as to call Evangelicalism "one of the two most important influences in Victorian society".[51]

It is obvious that these three main religious groups in Victorian England caused many rivalries amongst religious leaders, writers and society in general. The traditional church of England, Methodism and Evangelicalism differed from each other in many aspects, which often resulted in confrontation of opposing threads. Each stuck to their own interpretation of Christianity. While Methodists and Evangelicals believed in personal salvation the Anglican church promoted social reformation. Evangelicalism argued for a salvation "by grace through faith"[52], while Methodism taught salvation by works.[53] Methodists emphasised God's judgement, while Evangelicals stood by God's grace.[54]

6.2 The Brontës' faith

As indicated in a previous chapter, Charlotte Brontë was born into a family which set great store by religion. Her father Patrick Brontë was a clergyman and an Armenian Evangelical (Armenians' philosophy focused on free will). He was in the service of the Church of England but received his training by a "closely-knit group of Yorkshire Evangelicals".[55] Thus Charlotte was familiar with Christianity

---

[50] Cf. Ibid., 62.
[51] Quoted from: Ibid., p. 62
[52] Ephesians 2:8. The Bible. English Standard Version. Wheaton, Illinois: Crossway, 2006.
[53] Ibid., James 2:26.
[54] Cf. VanZanten Gallagher, Jane Eyre and Christianity, p. 63.
[55] Ibid., 62.

and its contents, as well as the Christian world-view demonstrated in the Bible. Her father in particular, adhered to a rather wider religious philosophy than perhaps the Anglican Church would have allowed, which he passed onto his children. In addition to the Brontës' open-mindedness, Charlotte also came into contact with the Methodist teachings through her aunt Branwell, who acted in the role of a guardian after her mother died. It is assumed that her aunt communicated to her a Calvinistic view of Christianity, emphasising a strict abstinence from sin and the fear of God's judgement. This scared the Brontë children and in later years Charlotte rather rejected a Calvinist interpretation of Christianity, endorsing a more liberal view of Christianity, evident from many passages in Jane Eyre.[56]

After the first publication of Jane Eyre, Charlotte had to face harsh criticism about the novel's irreligious and misleading nature. Many critics accused her of religious laxity and being a promoter of misleading teachings.[57] Viewing this as hypocrisy, close-mindedness and a lack of understanding the Bible, Charlotte responds in the author's preface to the second edition by saying:

> I would suggest to such doubters certain obvious distinctions; I would remind them of certain simple truths. Conventionality is not morality. Self-righteousness is not religion. To attack the first is to not assail the last. To pluck the mask from the face of the Pharisee is not to lift an impious hand to the Crown of Thorns. [...] Narrow human doctrines, that only tent to elate and magnify a few, should not be substituted for the world-redeeming creed of Christ. [58]

The following chapters include selected examples of Jane Eyre's religious criticism.

6.3 Mr. Brocklehurst

Mr Brocklehurst, who is the manager of Lowood school, marks Jane's first encounter with strong religious belief. Young Jane Eyre, upon their first meeting describes him as "a black pillar".[59] Jane's impression of him is one of terrible sternness and bitterness. He constantly concerns himself with the punishment

---

[56] Cf. Ibid., p. 62.
[57] Cf. Ibid., p. 62.
[58] Brontë, Charlotte (1897): Jane Eyre. Second edition. London: Service & Paton, preface.
[59] Brontë, Charlotte (2006): Jane Eyre. London: Penguin Group, p. 38.

and sin of children who disobey him.[60] This is highlighted by a small booklet Mr Brocklehurst hands to Jane which describes "an account of the awfully sudden death of Martha G., a naughty child addicted to falsehood and deceit".[61] In their very first encounter his conversation with Jane also contains much of the substance of his Christian belief. As Jane's Aunt Reed accuses her of being deceitful and false, Mr Brocklehurst replies:

> Your decisions are perfectly judicious, madam,' returned Mr Brocklehurst. 'Humility is a Christian grace, and one peculiarly appropriate to the pupils of Lowood; I, therefore, direct that special care shall be bestowed on its cultivation amongst them. I have studied how best to mortify in them the worldly sentiment of pride, and, only the other day, I had a pleasing proof of my success. My second daughter, Augusta, went with her mamma to visit the school, and on her return she exclaimed, "Oh, dear papa, how quiet and plain all the girls at Lowood look [...], they are almost like poor people's children!"[62]

Humility and humiliation mark the content of Mr Brocklehurst's Christian teaching. The simplicity of the pupils' dresses and a significant scene in chapter 7, in which he orders to have a girl's hair cut off, because it curls naturally, indicates a Calvinist belief. He implies a complete "sexual repression with a masculine and judgmental form of Christianity".[63] Charlotte Brontë here portrays a Calvinist Evangelical tradition that lacks one of the most fundamental Christians virtues: compassion.[64]

6.4 Helen Burns

A very different belief is embodied in the character of Helen Burns, a fellow pupil of Lowood school. Her understanding is of a compassionate, good God. In chapter 9, Helen replies to Jane's question, "Where is God? What is God?":

> My Maker and yours, who will never destroy what He created. I rely implicitly on His power, and confide wholly in His goodness: I count the hours till that eventful one arrives which shall restore me to Him, reveal Him to me. [...] I believe God is good; I can resign my immortal part to Him without any misgiving. God is my father; God is my friend: I love Him; I believe He loves me.[65]

---

[60] Cf. VanZanten Gallagher, Jane Eyre and Christianity, p. 65.
[61] Brontë, Jane Eyre, p. 42.
[62] Ibid., pp. 41.
[63] VanZanten Gallagher, Jane Eyre and Christianity, p. 65.
[64] Cf. Ibid., p. 65.
[65] Brontë, Jane Eyre, p.97.

In this crucial passage it becomes evident that Helen does not imagine God to have a judgmental nature. Even when she is close to dying, her thoughts are not directed towards the final judgement that the Bible dictates, but finds solace in a different feature in God's character: His goodness. This mild and positive interpretation and idea of a good and loving God that Helen embodies fascinates Jane. It is then (at Lowood) that Jane speaks her first prayer, asking for liberty, change and a new responsibility. Helen's view of Christianity influences her own faith. Helen's interpretation of Christianity represents liberal Evangelicalism which, like herself, focuses on God's love for all people.

6.5 Mr Rochester

One of the main characters, Mr Rochester, is not primarily linked with religion. He does nevertheless have a significant influence on Jane's spiritual life. He himself is of the opinion that people can form their own definition of morality or even be lax about it. His world-view does not consider Christianity, instead he formulates his own moral laws. Although Jane constantly defies his perception of religion and morality, she nonetheless undergoes a shift in her faith.[66] This is stated by herself in chapter 15:

> My future husband was becoming to me my whole world; and more than the world: almost my hope of heaven. He stood between me and every thought of religion, as an eclipse intervenes between man and the broad sun. I could not, in those days, see God for His creature: of whom I had made an idol.[67]

After Jane's and Mr Rochester's marriage is halted and her flight from Thornfield has already occurred, Mr Rochester himself witnesses a change of heart. Due to his despair at Jane's loss Jane he gradually turns to find comfort in God, whom he once renounced. Suddenly he begins to set great store by morality and even speaks of remorse:

> Of late, Jane—only—only of late—I began to see and acknowledge the hand of God in my doom. I began to experience remorse, repentance; the wish for reconcilement to my Maker. I began sometimes to pray: very brief prayers they were, but very sincere.[68]

---

[66] Cf. VanZanten Gallagher, Jane Eyre and Christianity, p. 65.
[67] Brontë, Jane Eyre, p. 316.
[68] Ibid., p. 501.

The religious transformation Mr Rochester experiences is one that reminds of a common phenomenon in Victorian society. Towards mid-century, Victorians adopted a certain moral laxity, due to the huge scientific progress which clashed with the teachings of the church. This moral laxity and, the so-called disappearance of God, evoked in many the wish for a return of religious values. In other parts this evolution aroused a religious renewal.[69] Mr Rochester went through exactly this transformation. He turned away from renouncing religious morals and renewed his spiritual life by believing in a Christian God.

6.6 St. John Rivers

The last religious representative is the clergyman St John Rivers, who saves Jane from death and offers her a place in his family home. His resemblance to Mr Rochester is striking. Like Mr Rochester, St. John proposes to Jane to marry him. There is a significant difference in these two proposals, which also indicates the difference in their faiths. "While Mr Rochester tempts Jane to give up God for love, St. John asks her to give up love and follow God"[70], as Susan VanZanten rightly puts it. Furthermore, in St. John, Jane again experiences a male desire for dominance over her life, as he pressures her into becoming his missionary wife.[71]

It is also necessary to compare him to Mr Brocklehurst. Both are members of the clergy, and both are seen by Jane as stern people who lack empathy. While Mr Brocklehurst is "a black pillar"[72], St. John is "a cold cumbrous column"[73]. St. John's perception of Christianity is a Calvinistic one, full of self-sacrifice and once again, directing its focus to a judgmental God. He repeatedly reminds Jane of the consequences awaiting her if she declines what is supposedly God's plan (accompanying him as a missionary to West India). As he falls in love with young Rosamond, he sternly renounces his feelings and instead decides to sacrifice himself in a life of religious servitude. St John's faith no doubt contains a new practical piety, which Evangelicalism stands for. Still, his Evangelicalism also

---

[69] cf. VanZanten Gallagher, Jane Eyre and Christianity, p. 62.
[70] Ibid., p.66
[71] Cf. Ibid., p. 66.
[72] Brontë, Jane Eyre p.38.
[73] Ibid., p. 465.

embodies stern Calvinistic traits which Jane and Charlotte Brontë both disliked, and which were very common amongst Victorians. [74]

6.7 Masculine and feminine images of God

Jane's encounters with male religious representatives suggest a strong and suppressive idea of God, with a cruel focus on sin and sexual abstinence. This religious tradition was quite common during the 19th century. On the other hand, the book presents a few female characters who provide a more positive model of Christian faith. Helen Burns, Miss Temple, Diana and Mary Rivers all believe in a compassionate God and liberal Christianity.[75] Jane also comes in direct contact with God as she cries for help, whereupon a supernatural and female voice responds: "My daughter, flee temptation".[76]

In her religious criticism, Charlotte Brontë deals with Christian concepts of self-sacrifice, authority, duty, and marriage. Her criticism is set towards a Christian male dominance and submission, as well as Calvinist interpretations. This justifies the conclusion that Jane Eyre can be rightfully called a "Christian feminist bildungsroman".[77]

---

[74] Cf. VanZanten Gallagher, Jane Eyre and Christianity, p. 66.
[75] Cf. Ibid., p. 67.
[76] Brontë, Jane Eyre, p. 367.
[77] Cf. VanZanten Gallagher, Jane Eyre and Christianity, p. 68.

7 Conclusion

What conclusion can be drawn from analysing and interpreting Jane Eyre in its historical context? Firstly, it is now evident how substantial Jane Eyre is when comparing it to given Victorian standards. The publication of the novel itself mirrors a denial of women's ability to produce art. Charlotte Brontë therefore published under an unambiguous pseudonym. In the novel itself, Jane reflects the social situation by actively being part of it. She herself is a member of the middle class, which was gaining on status. Being a woman, she faces all the oppression typical of the Victorian period. She does not 'sit still' and endure this suppression, however, but criticises it either by thought, speech or deed. Throughout her life she constantly seeks independence, which was not only untypical of a Victorian woman, but which was looked upon with contempt. Being intelligent and passionate she cannot identify herself with the image of womanhood valid at that time. Her morality dictates equality of gender. She makes up her own female mind when it comes to religion as well. Due to scientific progress the Victorian Era faced an emergence of many different interpretations of Christianity, Evangelicalism being the most influential amongst them. A repressive image of Christianity is presented to Jane by most of the male characters and she responses to this severe, Calvinistic idea of Christianity with criticism, affirming a just but nevertheless good God. Jane herewith presents us with examples of the developments and morals of the Victorians and revolts against what she finds unjust.

Bibliography

Print media

Monographies

Primary literature

Brontë, Charlotte (2006): Jane Eyre. London: Penguin Group.

Brontë, Charlotte (2007): Shirley. Oxford/New York: Oxford University Press.

The Bible. English Standard Version. Wheaton, Illinois: Crossway, 2006.

Brontë, Charlotte (1897): Jane Eyre. Second edition. London: Service & Paton.

Secondary literature

Paterson, Michael (2008): Life in Victorian Britain. A Social History of Queen Victoria's Reign. London: Robinson.

Roberts, Adam (2003): Victorian Culture and Society. London: Arnold, (The Essential Glossary series).

Burstyn, Joan N. (1980): Victorian education and the ideal of womenhood. London: Croom and Helm Ltd.

Academic papers

Bertolino, Paola (2001/2002): Female emancipation in Charlotte Bronte's Jane Eyre. Seminar paper. University of Leipzig.

Wilhelm, Beate (2005): The Role of Women in Victorian England reflected in Jane Eyre. Seminar paper. Albert-Ludwigs Universität Freiburg.

Kolle, Therese Cecilie (2011): Woman's struggle for autonomy. A reading of Jane Eyre, Wuthering Heights and The Mill on the Floss. MA Thesis. University of Oslo.

Peters, Cornelia (2016): Gender roles in Charlotte Brontë's "Jane Eyre".
Seminar paper. University of Koblenz-Landau.

De Groot, Caroline (2008): "Equal we are" - Jane Eyre Versus the Victorian
Woman. Seminar paper. Université catholique de Louvain.

Compilations

Erzgräber, Bernhard, Fabian/Kurt et al. (1991): Die Englische Literatur,
Epochen, Formen. Munich: Deutscher Taschenbuch Verlag.

Purchase, Sean (2006): Key Concepts in Victorian Literature. New York:
Palgrave Macmillian, (Palgrave Key Concepts: Literature).

VanZanten Gallagher, Susan (2001): Jane Eyre and Christianity. In: Long
Hoeveler, Diane/Lau, Beth: et al. (Ed.): Approaches to Teaching Charlotte
Brontë's Jane Eyre. New York: The Modern Language Association of America.
(Approaches to Teaching World Literature)

Magazines/Journals

Besant, Walter (1897): Jubilee Portrait of our Queen. In: Illustrated London
News. Diamond Jubilee number.

Khan, Tahir Amin (2017): Social classes in Victorian Era. In: International
Journal of Advance Engineering and Research Development. Vol. 4. Iss. 7

Online sources

Online dictionaries

Oxford Dictionary (2019): Bildungsroman. URL:
https://en.oxforddictionaries.com/definition/bildungsroman (accessed
February 17th 2019)

Oxford Dictionary: Feminism. URL:
https://en.oxforddictionaries.com/definition/feminism (accessed February
14th 2019)